MICROSOFT

AZURE

AI-900

Learn The Basics in One Day

By

Dr Issa Ngoie

DEDICATION

This book is dedicated to the memory of my brother **Ali Kandeke Lumena**, my **oncle Marcel Bitobe** and my beloved mother **Kabibi Mukemwendo Lumande**.

While their lives on this earth was entirely too short, I am certain that with their zest for life, energetic personalities, curious natures, and kinds and compassionate hearts their truly would have made a great impact on this world.

There's Nothing New Under the Sun

What has been will be again,

What has been done will be done again;

There is nothing new under the sun.

Is there anything of which one can say?

"Look! This is something new"?

It was here already long ago;

It was here before our time.

– Ecclesiastes 1:9-10

Artificial = Made or produced by human being.

Artificial = Not occurring naturally.

Artificial = Copy of something natural.

Intelligence = _The ability to acquire, apply knowledge.

Artificial + Intelligence

⇓

Ability to produce something similar by human being

Introduction to AI

AI enables us to build amazing software that can improve health care, enable people to overcome physical disadvantages, empower smart infrastructure, create incredible entertainment experiences, and even save the planet!

What is AI?

Simply put, AI is software that imitates human behaviors and capabilities. Key workloads include:

- **Machine learning** – This is often the foundation for an AI system, and is the way we "teach" a computer model to make predictions and draw conclusions from data.

Machine=A device that applies force, changes the direction of a force, or changes the strength of a force, in order to perform a task, generally involving work done on a load.

Learning=a process that leads to change, which occurs as a result of experience and increases the potential for improved performance and future learning

Machine + Learning = A device that learns from experience .

- **Computer vision** – Capabilities within AI to interpret the world visually through cameras, video, and images.

Computer + Vision= Enable Computer to make decision from data received from cameras,video,...

Exercises

1.What is artificial ?
2. what is intelligence?
3. what is artificial intelligence?
4. what is a machine?
5. what is machine learning?
6. list some benefits of using artificial intelligence.

Definition 2 : *Computer vision* is a field of computer science that focuses on enabling computers to identify and understand objects and people in images and videos.

- **Natural language processing** – Capabilities within AI for a computer to interpret written or spoken language, and respond in kind.

- **Document intelligence** – Capabilities within AI that deal with managing, processing, and using high volumes of data found in forms and documents.

- **Knowledge mining** – Capabilities within AI to extract information from large volumes of often unstructured data to create a searchable knowledge store.
- **Generative AI** – Capabilities within AI that create original content in a variety of formats including natural language, image, code, and more.

Exercise

1. What is computer vision
2. List some applications of generative AI
3. What is Knowledge mining?

Machine Learning

Machine Learning is the foundation for most AI solutions. **Since the 1950's**, researchers, often known as *data scientists*, have worked on different approaches to AI. Most modern applications of AI have their origins in machine learning, a branch of AI that combines computer science and mathematics.

Let's start by looking at a real-world example of how machine learning can be used to solve a difficult problem.

Sustainable farming techniques are essential to maximize food production while protecting a fragile environment. *The Yield*, an agricultural technology company based in Australia, uses sensors, data, and machine learning to help farmers make informed decisions related to weather, soil, and plant conditions.

How machine learning works

How Do Machines Learn?

The answer is, from data. In today's world, we create huge volumes of data as we go about our everyday lives. From the text messages, emails, and social media posts we send to the photographs and videos we take on our phones, we generate massive amounts of information. More data still is created by millions of sensors in our homes, cars, cities, public transport infrastructure, and factories.

Data scientists can use all of that data to train machine learning models that can make predictions and inferences based on the relationships they find in the data.

Machine learning models try to capture the relationship between data. For example, suppose an environmental conservation organization wants volunteers to identify and catalog different species of wildflower using a phone app. The following animation shows how machine learning can be used to enable this scenario.

1. A team of botanists and scientists collect data on wildflower samples.
2. The team labels the samples with the correct species.

3. The labeled data is processed using an algorithm that finds relationships between the features of the samples and the labeled species.
4. The results of the algorithm are encapsulated in a model.
5. When new samples are found by volunteers, the model can identify the correct species label.

Approaches to AI have advanced to complete tasks of much greater complexity. These complex models form the basis of AI capabilities.

Machine learning in Microsoft Azure

Microsoft Azure provides the **Azure Machine Learning** service – a cloud-based platform for creating, managing, and publishing machine learning models. **Azure Machine Learning**

Studio offers multiple authoring experiences such as:

- **Automated machine learning**: this feature enables non-experts to quickly create an effective machine learning model from data.
- **Azure Machine Learning designer**: a graphical interface enabling no-code development of machine learning solutions.
- **Data metric visualization**: analyze and optimize your experiments with visualization.
- **Notebooks**: write and run your own code in managed Jupyter Notebook servers that are directly integrated in the studio.

Exercise

1. What can we do with automated machine learning?
2. Explain how machine learning is used in azure.

3. What is labelled data
4. What is supervised learning?
5. What is trained data?

computer vision

Computer Vision is an area of AI that deals with visual processing. Let's explore some of the possibilities that computer vision brings.

The **Seeing AI** app is a great example of the power of computer vision. Designed for the blind and low vision community, the Seeing AI app harnesses the power of AI to open up the visual world and describe nearby people, text and objects.

Computer Vision models and capabilities

Most computer vision solutions are based on machine learning models that can be applied to visual input from cameras, videos, or images. The following table describes common computer vision tasks.

Expand table

Task	Description
Image classification	 Image classification involves training a machine learning model to classify images based on their contents. For example, in a traffic monitoring solution you might use an image classification model to classify images based on the type of vehicle they contain, such as taxis, buses, cyclists, and so on.
Object detection	 Object detection machine learning models are trained to classify individual objects within an image, and identify their location with a bounding box. For example, a traffic monitoring solution might use object detection to identify the location of different classes of vehicle.
Semantic segmentation	

Semantic segmentation is an advanced machine learning technique in which individual pixels in the image are classified according to the object to which they belong. For example, a traffic monitoring solution might overlay traffic images with "mask" layers to highlight different vehicles using specific colors.

Image analysis

You can create solutions that combine machine learning models with advanced image analysis techniques to extract information from images, including "tags" that could help catalog the image or even descriptive captions that summarize the scene shown in the image.

Face detection, analysis, and recognition

Face detection is a specialized form of object detection that locates human faces in an image. This can be combined with classification and facial geometry analysis techniques to recognize individuals based on their facial features.

Optical character recognition (OCR)

Optical character recognition is a technique used to detect and read text in images. You can use OCR to read text in photographs (for example, road signs or store fronts) or to extract information from scanned documents such as letters, invoices, or forms.

Computer vision services in Microsoft Azure

You can use Microsoft's **Azure AI Vision** to develop computer vision solutions. The service features are available for use and testing in the **Azure Vision Studio** and other programming languages. Some features of Azure AI Vision include:

- **Image Analysis**: capabilities for analyzing images and video, and extracting descriptions, tags, objects, and text.
- **Face**: capabilities that enable you to build face detection and facial recognition solutions.
- **Optical Character Recognition (OCR)**: capabilities for extracting printed or handwritten text from images, enabling access to a digital version of the scanned text.

Natural Language Processing

Natural language processing (NLP) is the area of AI that deals with creating software that understands written and spoken language.

NLP enables you to create software that can:

- Analyze and interpret text in documents, email messages, and other sources.
- Interpret spoken language, and synthesize speech responses.
- Automatically translate spoken or written phrases between languages.
- Interpret commands and determine appropriate actions.

For example, *Starship Commander* is a virtual reality (VR) game from Human Interact that takes place in a science fiction world. The game uses natural language processing to enable players to control the narrative and interact with in-game characters and starship systems.

Natural language processing in Microsoft Azure

You can use Microsoft's **Azure AI Language** to build natural language processing solutions. Some features of Azure AI Language include understanding and analyzing text, training conversational language models that can understand spoken or text-based commands, and building intelligent applications.

Microsoft's **Azure AI Speech** is another service that can be used to build natural language processing solutions. Azure AI Speech features include speech recognition and synthesis, real-time translations, conversation transcriptions, and more.

You can explore Azure AI Language features in the **Azure Language Studio** and Azure AI

Speech features in the **Azure Speech Studio**. The service features are available for use and testing in the studios and other programming languages.

Document intelligence and knowledge mining

Document Intelligence is the area of AI that deals with managing, processing, and using high volumes of a variety of data found in forms and documents. Document intelligence enables you to create software that can automate processing for contracts, health documents, financial forms and more

Document intelligence in Microsoft Azure

You can use Microsoft's **Azure AI Document Intelligence** to build solutions that manage and accelerate data collection from scanned documents. Features of Azure AI Document Intelligence help automate document processing in applications and workflows, enhance data-driven strategies, and enrich document search capabilities. You can use prebuilt models to add intelligent document processing for invoices, receipts, health insurance cards, tax forms, and more. You can also use Azure AI Document Intelligence to create custom models with your own labeled datasets. The service features are available for use and testing in the **Document Intelligence Studio** and other programming languages.

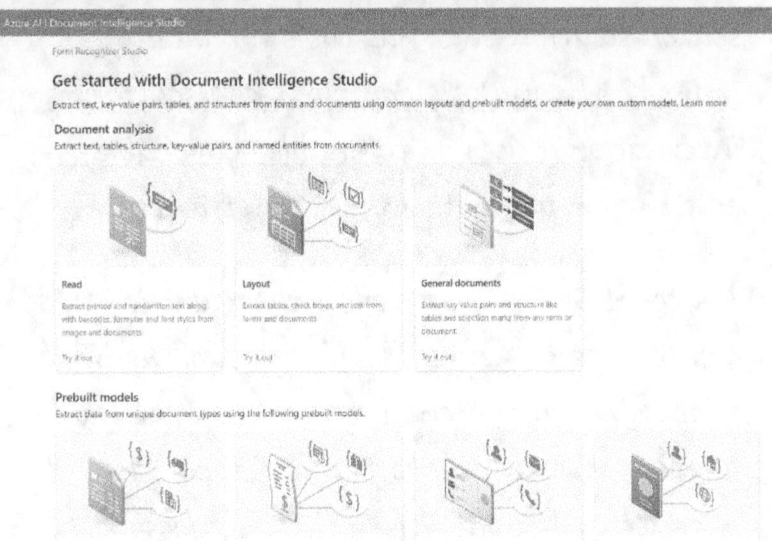

Knowledge Mining

Knowledge mining is the term used to describe solutions that involve extracting information from large volumes of often unstructured data to create a searchable knowledge store.

Knowledge mining in Microsoft Azure

One Microsoft knowledge mining solution is **Azure AI Search**, a private, enterprise, search solution that has tools for building indexes. The indexes can then be used for internal only use, or to enable searchable content on public facing internet assets.

Azure AI Search can utilize the built-in AI capabilities of Azure AI services such as image processing, document intelligence, and natural language processing to extract data. The product's AI capabilities makes it possible to index previously unsearchable documents and to extract and surface insights from large amounts of data quickly.

Understand generative AI

Generative AI describes a category of capabilities within AI that create original content. People typically interact with generative AI that has been built into chat applications. Generative AI applications take in natural language input, and return appropriate responses in a variety of formats including natural language, image, code, and audio.

Generative AI in Microsoft Azure

In Microsoft Azure, you can use the **Azure OpenAI service** to build generative AI solutions. Azure OpenAI Service is Microsoft's cloud solution for deploying, customizing, and hosting generative AI models. It brings together the best of OpenAI's cutting edge models and APIs with the security and scalability of the Azure cloud platform.

Azure OpenAI supports many foundation model choices that can serve different needs. The service features are available for use and testing in the **Azure OpenAI Studio** and other programming languages. You can use the Azure OpenAI Studio user interface to manage, develop, and customize generative AI models.

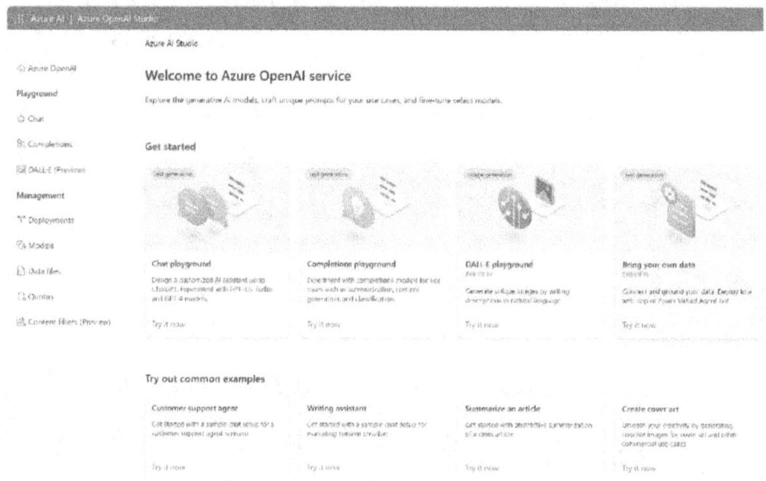

Challenges and risks with AI

Artificial Intelligence is a powerful tool that can be used to greatly benefit the world. However, like any tool, it must be used responsibly.

The following table shows some of the potential challenges and risks facing an AI application developer.

Challenge or Risk	Example
Bias can affect results	A loan-approval model discriminates by gender due to bias in the data with which it was trained
Errors may cause harm	An autonomous vehicle experiences a system failure and causes a collision
Data could be exposed	A medical diagnostic bot is trained using sensitive patient data, which is stored insecurely
Solutions may not work for everyone	A home automation assistant provides no audio output for visually impaired users
Users must trust a complex system	An AI-based financial tool makes investment recommendations - what are they based on?
Who's liable for AI-driven decisions?	An innocent person is convicted of a crime based on evidence from facial recognition – who's responsible?

Understand Responsible AI

At Microsoft, AI software development is guided by a set of six principles, designed to ensure that AI applications provide amazing solutions to difficult problems without any unintended negative consequences.

Fairness

AI systems should treat all people fairly. For example, suppose you create a machine learning model to support a loan approval application for a bank. The model should predict whether the loan should be approved or denied without bias. This bias could be based on gender, ethnicity, or other factors that result in an unfair advantage or disadvantage to specific groups of applicants.

Azure Machine Learning includes the capability to interpret models and quantify the extent to which each feature of the data influences the model's prediction. This capability helps data scientists and developers identify and mitigate bias in the model.

Another example is Microsoft's implementation of <u>Responsible AI with the Face service</u>, which retires facial recognition capabilities that can be used to try to infer emotional states and identity attributes. These capabilities, if misused, can subject people to stereotyping, discrimination or unfair denial of services.

Reliability and safety

AI systems should perform reliably and safely. For example, consider an AI-based software system for an autonomous vehicle; or a machine learning model that diagnoses patient symptoms and recommends prescriptions. Unreliability in these kinds of systems can result in substantial risk to human life.

AI-based software application development must be subjected to rigorous testing and deployment management processes to ensure that they work as expected before release.

Privacy and security

AI systems should be secure and respect privacy. The machine learning models on which AI systems are based rely on large volumes of data, which may contain personal details that must be kept private. Even after the models are trained and the system is in production, privacy and security need to be considered. As the system uses new data to make predictions or take action, both the data and decisions made from the data may be subject to privacy or security concerns.

Inclusiveness

AI systems should empower everyone and engage people. AI should bring benefits to all parts of society, regardless of physical ability, gender, sexual orientation, ethnicity, or other factors.

Transparency

AI systems should be understandable. Users should be made fully aware of the purpose of the system, how it works, and what limitations may be expected.

Accountability

People should be accountable for AI systems. Designers and developers of AI-based solutions should work within a framework of governance and organizational principles that ensure the solution meets ethical and legal standards that are clearly defined.

The principles of responsible AI can help you understand some of the challenges facing developers as they try to create ethical AI solutions.

AI Terms

From <u>edge AI computing</u> to <u>reinforcement learning</u>, artificial intelligence (AI) is a field filled with technical terms. It can be difficult to pin down exactly what a term means, particularly if you don't work directly with data every day.

That's why we've created a glossary of 50 AI terms that frequently come up in discussions about AI and machine learning. If you can lock down these basics, you should be able to hold your own in any discussion about machine learning. Let's run through them in alphabetical order.

Algorithm: A set of rules that a machine can follow to learn how to do a task.

Artificial intelligence: This refers to the general concept of machines acting in a way that simulates or mimics human intelligence. AI can have a variety of features, such as human-like communication or decision making.

Autonomous: A machine is described as autonomous if it can perform its task or tasks without needing human intervention.

Backward chaining: A method where the model starts with the desired output and works in reverse to find data that might support it.

Bias: Assumptions made by a model that simplify the process of learning to do its assigned task. Most supervised machine learning models perform better with low <u>bias</u>, as these assumptions can negatively affect results.

Big data: Datasets that are too large or complex to be used by traditional data processing applications.

Bounding box: Commonly used in image or video tagging, this is an imaginary box drawn on visual information. The contents of the box are labeled to help a model recognize it as a distinct type of object.

Chatbot: A <u>chatbot</u> is program that is designed to communicate with people through text or voice commands in a way that mimics human-to-human conversation.

Cognitive computing: This is effectively another way to say artificial intelligence. It's used by marketing teams at some companies to avoid the science fiction aura that sometimes surrounds AI.

Computational learning theory: A field within artificial intelligence that is primarily concerned with creating and analyzing machine learning algorithms.

Corpus: A large dataset of written or spoken material that can be used to train a machine to perform linguistic tasks.

Data mining: The process of analyzing datasets in order to discover new patterns that might improve the model.

Data science: Drawing from statistics, computer science and information science, this interdisciplinary field aims to use a variety of scientific methods, processes and systems to solve problems involving data.

Dataset: A collection of related data points, usually with a uniform order and tags.

Deep learning: A function of artificial intelligence that imitates the human brain by learning from the way data is structured, rather than from an algorithm that's programmed to do one specific thing.

Entity annotation: The process of labeling unstructured sentences with information so that a machine can read them. This could involve labeling all people, organizations and locations in a document, for example.

Entity extraction: An umbrella term referring to the process of adding structure to data so that a machine can read it. _Entity extraction_ may be done by humans or by a machine learning model.

Forward chaining: A method in which a machine must work from a problem to find a potential solution. By analyzing a range of hypotheses, the AI must determine those that are relevant to the problem.

General AI: AI that could successfully do any intellectual task that can be done by any human being. This is sometimes referred to as *strong AI*, although they aren't entirely equivalent terms.

Hyperparameter: Occasionally used interchangeably with *parameter*, although the terms have some subtle differences. Hyperparameters are values that affect the way your model learns. They are usually set manually outside the model.

Intent: Commonly used in training data for chatbots and other natural language processing tasks, this is a type of label that defines the purpose or goal of what is said. For example, the intent for the phrase "turn the volume down" could be "decrease volume".

Label: A part of training data that identifies the desired output for that particular piece of data.

Linguistic annotation: Tagging a dataset of sentences with the subject of each sentence, ready for some form of analysis or assessment. Common uses for linguistically annotated data include sentiment analysis and natural language processing.

Machine intelligence: An umbrella term for various types of learning algorithms, including machine learning and deep learning.

Machine learning: This subset of AI is particularly focused on developing algorithms that will help machines to learn and change in response to new data, without the help of a human being.

Machine translation: The translation of text by an algorithm, independent of any human involvement.

Model: A broad term referring to the product of AI training, created by running a machine learning algorithm on training data.

Neural network: Also called a *neural net*, a neural network is a computer system designed to function like the human brain. Although researchers are still working on creating a machine model of the human brain, existing <u>neural networks</u> can perform many tasks involving speech, vision and board game strategy.

Natural language generation (NLG): This refers to the process by which a machine turns structured data into text or speech that humans can understand. Essentially, NLG is concerned with what a machine writes or says as the end part of the communication process.

Natural language processing (NLP): The umbrella term for any machine's ability to perform conversational tasks, such as recognizing what is said to it, understanding the intended meaning and responding intelligibly.

Natural language understanding (NLU): As a subset of natural language processing, natural language understanding deals with helping machines to recognize the intended meaning of language — taking into account its subtle nuances and any grammatical errors.

Overfitting: An important AI term, overfitting is a symptom of machine learning training in which an algorithm is only able to work on or identify specific examples present in the training data. A working model should be able to use the general trends behind the data to work on new examples.

Parameter: A variable inside the model that helps it to make predictions. A parameter's value can be estimated using data and they are usually not set by the person running the model.

Pattern recognition: The distinction between pattern recognition and machine learning is often blurry, but this field is basically concerned with finding trends and patterns in data.

Predictive analytics: By combining data mining and machine learning, this type of analytics is built to forecast what will happen within a given timeframe based on historical data and trends.

Python: A popular programming language used for general programming.

Reinforcement learning: A method of teaching AI that sets a goal without specific metrics, encouraging the model to test different scenarios rather than find a single answer. Based on human feedback, the model can then manipulate the next scenario to get better results.

Semantic annotation: Tagging different search queries or products with the goal of improving the relevance of a search engine.

Sentiment analysis: The process of _identifying and categorizing opinions_ in a piece of text, often with the goal of determining the writer's attitude towards something.

Strong AI: This field of research is focused on developing AI that is equal to the human mind when it comes to ability. _General AI_ is a similar term often used interchangeably.

Supervised learning: This is a type of machine learning where structured datasets, with inputs and labels, are used to train and develop an algorithm.

Test data: The unlabeled data used to check that a machine learning model is able to perform its assigned task.

Training data: This refers to all of the data used during the process of training a machine learning algorithm, as well as the specific dataset used for training rather than testing.

Transfer learning: This method of learning involves spending time teaching a machine to do a related task, then allowing it to return to its original work with improved accuracy. One potential example of this is taking a model that analyzes sentiment in product reviews and asking it to analyze tweets for a week.

Turing test: Named after Alan Turing, famed mathematician, computer scientist and logician, this tests a machine's ability to pass for a human, particularly in the fields of language and behavior. After being graded by a human, the machine passes if its output is indistinguishable from that of human participant's.

Unsupervised learning: This is a form of training where the algorithm is asked to make inferences from datasets that don't contain labels. These inferences are what help it to learn.

Validation data: Structured like training data with an input and labels, this data is used to test a recently trained model against new data and to analyze performance, with a particular focus on checking for overfitting.

Variance: The amount that the intended function of a machine learning model changes while it's being trained. Despite being flexible, models with high variance are prone to overfitting and low predictive accuracy because they are reliant on their <u>training data</u>.

Variation: Also called *queries* or *utterances*, these work in tandem with intents for natural language processing. The variation is what a person might say to achieve a certain purpose or goal. For example, if the intent is "pay by credit card," the variation might be "I'd like to pay by card, please."

Weak AI: Also called *narrow AI*, this is a model that has a set range of skills and focuses on one particular set of tasks. Most AI currently in use is weak AI, unable to learn or perform tasks outside of its specialist skill set.